MAJESTY

Text • Jodi Parry Belknap   Design • Momi Cazimero, Graphic House, Inc.   Development & Marketing • Nancy E. Lewis   Photography • Douglas Peebles

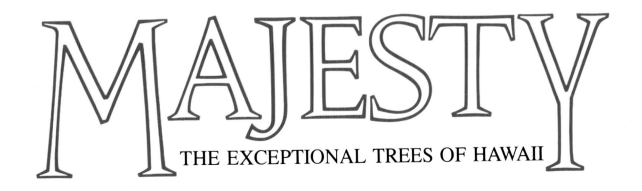

MAJESTY
THE EXCEPTIONAL TREES OF HAWAII

PUBLISHED BY

THE OUTDOOR CIRCLE

HONOLULU, HAWAII

1982

Designed and typeset in Honolulu, Hawaii
Printed and bound in Hong Kong

ISBN 0-9609082-0-X
Library of Congress No. 82-60598

Preface

THE OUTDOOR CIRCLE is a non-profit organization founded in Hawaii in 1912 to preserve the natural beauty of the islands. The considerable achievements of its volunteer members in the years since have helped make Hawaii one of the loveliest places in the world in which to live. The organization's most significant accomplishments include an instrumental role in establishing legislation in 1927 banning billboards in Hawaii, the planting of tens of thousands of shade and ornamental trees along streets and avenues and in public places in the islands, the initiation of youth environmental education programs, and the continued protection of Hawaii's great number of rare and unusual trees. With the publication of this book, The Outdoor Circle celebrates its 70th anniversary.

Presidents responsible for guiding The Outdoor Circle through the past 70 years and taking the major role in maintaining its degree of effectiveness include:

Mrs. Frederick J. Lowrey
Mrs. L.A. Thurston
Mrs. A.A. Young
Mrs. A.G.M. Robertson
Mrs. F.R. Day
Miss Beatrice Castle
Mrs. C.B. Cooper
Mrs. B.E. Newcomb
Mrs. Walter F. Dillingham
Mrs. Theo. A. Cooke
Mrs. Charles Chillingworth
Mrs. Frederick D. Lowrey
Mrs. Robert E. White
Mrs. Wayne Pfleuger
Mrs. E.E. Black
Mrs. Peter K. McLean
Mrs. Alice Spalding Bowen
Mrs. Florence Broadbent
Mrs. Bartley Harloe
Mrs. Harlan F. Benner
Mrs. Fred Wolf
Mrs. Frank Broadbent
Mrs. Janet Wimberly
Mrs. Alan S. Davis
Mrs. Charles H. Davis
Mrs. Jack Marnie
Mrs. William Blackfield
Mrs. Richard H. Rice
Mrs. Harold R. Erdman
Mrs. Robert T. Sasaki
Mrs. John G. Simpson
Mrs. Bob Hargreaves
Mrs. Harold Eichelberger
Mrs. Robert Creps
Mrs. Ashby J. Fristoe
Mrs. John T. Humme
Mrs. Theodore Crocker
Mrs. William McKeever
Mrs. Arthur Stubenberg

The publisher wishes to express its deep felt appreciation to those who have contributed to the support of this publication.

Atherton Family Foundation
Everett E. Black, Sr.
Mrs. George O. Burr
Samuel N. & Mary Castle Foundation
Zipporah B. Douglas
Frear Eleemosynary Trust
Gladys Q. Knapp
Loy M. Marks
McInerny Foundation
Pacific Beach Hotel and
    Pagoda Hotel & Restaurant
Pan American Airways
Drs. Leonard & Evelyn Richie
The G. N. Wilcox Trust

Foreword

The legacy of Hawaii's exceptional trees is rooted in the epic period of Polynesian migration to these islands that began over a thousand years ago. The pattern of transporting useful plants to ensure a more comfortable and productive life in the new land was repeated more extensively a few centuries later when waves of new immigrants from both East and West began arriving in Hawaii.

At the beginning of the nineteenth century a Spaniard, Don Francisco de Paula Marin, landed in Honolulu from Mexico to become a gardener and vineyard keeper. Among the many food plants he introduced now commonly found in island markets as well as naturalized in fields and along roadsides, were new fruit trees.

At mid-century interest in the importation of plants was given great impetus by Hawaii's burgeoning role as a transpacific trade center. Supported by local businessmen, King Kamehameha III set up an experimental plant import garden and, with the help of the royal physician and botanist, Dr. William Hillebrand, began a thoughtful introduction of trees with economic potential from the world's tropics, trees that would be useful for food, ship building, and general construction in the rapidly growing village of Honolulu.

Often during this period, voyagers arriving from distant ports brought seeds for new trees with them in shipments such as the one containing fruits and medicinal plants from the Orient accompanying the first Chinese immigrants to Hawaii in 1852. The introduction of new trees continued throughout the century. Many other individuals— businessmen, sea-captains, and housewives determined to have bountiful orchards—obtained new tree seeds and seedlings for Hawaii's gardens.

Shortly after the beginning of the twentieth century, a far more extensive program of plant importation was undertaken by the Hawaii Sugar Planters' Association (HSPA) under the leadership of a noted botanist, Harold L. Lyon. The two-fold goal was to ensure the continued availability of water to Hawaii's sugar industry and to provide economically viable tree crops. This was accomplished by reforesting lowland and midland marginal lands important for watershed and soil conservation. H.S.P.A. imports totalled nearly 10,000 species which were distributed to arborists throughout Hawaii. Three of the central experimental planting stations used for the project are well-known in Hawaii today as Foster Botanic Garden in downtown Honolulu, Lyon Arboretum in Manoa Valley, and Wahiawa Botanic Garden in central Oahu.

The massive plantings were augmented by other individuals—territorial foresters and private citizens—who introduced additional trees with economic potential. The new trees flourished in Hawaii's rich volcanic soil. Today, many formerly barren parts of the islands are cloaked in green.

In 1974 the Mokihana Club, a small but dedicated and determined citizens' group on the island of Kauai, rallied community support to prevent destruction of an exceptionally large and beautiful banyan tree on the island. From this effort grew the realization that legislation was needed to protect similar trees throughout the state. This was obtained in 1975 when the Hawaii State Legislature passed Act 105 (Chapter 58, Hawaii Revised Statutes) mandating each County to establish a County Arborist Advisory Committee composed of five knowledgeable citizens appointed by the Mayors of each County. Citizens on the garden island of Kauai already had taken the lead by passing a protective ordinance on December 27, 1974. The Outdoor Circle was prominent among citizens' groups urging support of the legislation.

To date twelve exceptional trees have been protected by ordinance on the island of Kauai; one hundred and two are protected by Oahu's 1978 ordinance. Tree selections for designation as 'exceptional' are based on nominations presented by citizens or citizens' groups to the County Arborist Advisory Committees. Trees are evaluated on the basis of age, rarity, location, size, aesthetic quality, endemic status, or historic and cultural significance.

The exceptional trees in this book represent a vital and majestic part of Hawaii's heritage. They are a living legacy from those early generations of pioneer men and women who settled Hawaii, a legacy to be appreciated by present generations and lovingly conserved for future generations.

Paul R. Weissich, Director,
Honolulu Botanic Gardens

Act 105

Enacted by the Legislature of the State of Hawaii

PURPOSE

The purpose of this Act is to provide for better environmental control in order to improve the quality of life in the State. The state and county governments have a duty to enhance, whenever and wherever possible, the natural environment of our State.

The legislature finds that rapid physical and economic development has led to the destruction of many of the State's exceptional trees, as well as to the near-extinction of several such trees. Further, the legislature finds that, beyond their esthetic worth and cultural significance, trees perform an important role in maintaining ecological balance, in increasing soil conservation and natural oxygen production, as wind breaks for necessary plant species, and in retarding flooding, erosion, siltation, lateral distribution of air pollutants, and noise.

Short-sighted land development, which strips the land of its essential vegetation and trees, upsets a vital ecological balance, endangers new occupants of the land, and decreases natural beauty. Thus, encouragement of enlightened trees, and appropriate land development controls to prevent removal and destruction of exceptional trees are urgently needed. The purpose of this Act is to require the counties, who possess primary control over land development, to enact protective regulations to safeguard exceptional trees.

COUNTY ARBORIST ADVISORY COMMITTEES

Each county of the State shall establish a county arborist advisory committee, which shall be appointed by the mayor and shall include the county planning director, or his designee; one member who shall be actively employed in the practice of landscape architecture, and not less that three other members selected on the basis of active participation in programs of community beautification, or research or organization in the ecological sciences, including ethnobotany, or Hawaiiana.

POWERS AND DUTIES

For the purposes of this chapter, the county committees shall have the following powers and duties in addition to those delegated by the respective county councils.

(1) To research, prepare, and recommend to the county council exceptional trees to be protected by county ordinance or regulation.
(2) To advise property owners relative to the preservation and enhancement of exceptional trees.
(3) To recommend to the county council appropriate protective ordinances, regulations, and procedures.
(4) To review all actions deemed by the county council to endanger exceptional trees.

For the purposes of this section, "exceptional trees" means a tree or stand or grove of trees with historic or cultural value, or which by reason of its age, rarity, location, size, esthetic quality, or endemic status has been designated by the county committee as worthy of preservation. Exceptional trees may be designated generally by biotaxy or individually by location or class.

COUNTY PROTECTIVE REGULATIONS

Each county shall enact appropriate protective regulations which designate exceptional trees, whether by removal or the existence of conditions which lead to the destruction of such trees; provide for site plan review and amendment to protect exceptional trees; and provide for injunctive relief against the removal or destruction of exceptional trees.

STATE ASSISTANCE

The department of land and natural resources, the University of Hawaii, and the Hawaii foundation for history and the humanities shall cooperate with and to the fullest extent possible assist the counties and their respective committees in carrying out this chapter.

(Excerpts from Act 105 approved May 17, 1975.)

Oahu County Arborist Advisory Committee
Dorothy Hargreaves, Chairman
Susan L. Fristoe
Erling E. Hedemann Jr.
Robert B. Jones
Han Sam Yee

Kauai County Arborist Advisory Committee
Ralph Daehler, Chairman
Avery Youn, Vice Chairman
John G. Allerton
Francis Takahashi

Register of Exceptional Trees

County of Oahu

Adansonia digitata, Baobab Tree*
1301 Punchbowl Street, Queen's Medical Center

Adansonia digitata, Baobab Tree
Ala Moana Park

+ **Agathis robusta, Kauri Tree***
Foster Botanic Garden

++ **Agathis robusta, Kauri Tree**
Harold L. Lyon Arboretum

Agathis robusta, Kauri Tree
Judiciary Building, Ewa Courtyard

○ **Anacardium occidentale, Cashew Nut Tree***
Kaneohe Ranch

○ **Araucaria bidwilii, Bunya Bunya Tree***
Kaneohe Ranch

++ **Araucaria cunninghamii, Hoop Pine Tree**
Harold L. Lyon Arboretum

+ **Araucaria cunninghamii, Hoop Pine Tree**
Foster Botanic Garden

○ **Araucaria excelsa, Norfolk Island Pine Tree***
Kaneohe Ranch

Arecastrum romanzoffianum, Queens Palm
row of 10, 1071 Young Street

○ **Artocarpus incisus, Breadfruit Tree***
Kaneohe Ranch

○○ **Bertholletia excelsa, Brazil Nut Tree***
Walker Garden

Bombax malabaricum, Red Silk Cotton Tree
Queen's Medical Center

Bucida buceras, Geometry Tree*
Ala Moana Park

+ **Bumelia buxifolia, Ironwood Tree**
Foster Botanic Garden

Calophyllum inophyllum, Kamani Tree*
Kualoa Regional Park—corner near Fishpond, makai
of Kamehameha Highway

+ **Canarium commune, Pili Nut Tree**
Foster Botanic Garden

Canarium vulgare, Pili Nut Trees*
two trees, Washington Place

++ **Caryota cumingii, Fishtail Palm**
Harold L. Lyon Arboretum

Caryota urens, Wine Palm
Wahiawa Botanic Garden, 1396 California Avenue

Casuarina equisetifolia, Ironwood Tree*
along Kalakaua Avenue from Kapahulu Avenue to
Poni Moi Road

+ **Catalpa longissima, Yoke Wood Tree**
Foster Botanic Garden

+ **Cavanillesia platanifolia, Quipo Tree***
Foster Botanic Garden

Cecropia obtusifolia, Trumpet Tree
Paradise Park, 3737 Manoa Road

Ceiba pentandra, Kapok Tree
Grounds of State Department of Agriculture
1428 South King Street

+ **Ceiba pentandra, Kapok Trees***
Foster Botanic Garden

+ **Couroupita guianensis, Cannonball Tree***
Foster Botanic Garden

Couroupita guianensis, Cannonball Tree
University of Hawaii, Manoa Campus

++ **Cyrtostachys lakka, Sealing Wax Palm**
Harold L. Lyon Arboretum

○ **Delonix regia, Royal Poinciana Tree***
Kaneohe Ranch

+ **Elaedodendron orientale, False Olive Tree***
Foster Botanic Garden

Enterolobium cyclocarpum, Earpod Tree
Honolulu Zoo, 151 Kapahulu Avenue

Enterolobium cyclocarpum, Earpod Tree
Board of Water Supply, Makiki Pumping Station

+ **Enterolobium cyclocarpum, Earpod Tree**
Foster Botanic Garden

Enterolobium cyclocarpum, Earpod Tree
Grounds of State Department of Agriculture
1428 South King Street

Enterolobium cyclocarpum, Earpod Tree
Waialua, in front of old Post Office

+ **Erythrina sandwicensis, Wili-wili Trees***
Foster Botanic Garden at Koko Crater.

Eucalyptus deglupta, Mindanao Gum Tree*
Wahiawa Botanic Garden, 1396 California Avenue

○ **Eugenia malaccensis, Mountain Apple Tree***
Kaneohe Ranch

Ficus, spp. Banyan Trees, *(collection)*
Ala Moana Park

Ficus benghalensis, Banyan Tree*
Iolani Palace Grounds

Ficus benghalensis, Banyan Tree*
Moana Hotel Courtyard, 2365 Kalakaua Avenue

Ficus benghalensis, Banyan Tree
Kuhio Beach Park

Ficus benghalensis, Banyan Trees
two beside Judiciary Building

Ficus benghalensis, Banyan Tree
Parking Lot Walina Street, The Food Pantry Ltd.,
2370 Kuhio Avenue

Ficus elastica, Indian Rubber Tree
University of Hawaii, Manoa campus,
next to Campus Way, mauka side of Sinclair Library

Ficus macrophylla, Moreton Bay Fig Tree*
Queen Emma Square

Ficus religiosa, Bo Tree*
Moanalua Gardens, 1352 Pineapple Place

○○ **Ficus religiosa, Bo Tree**
Walker Garden

Ficus religiosa, Bo Tree
University of Hawaii, Manoa campus,
mauka end of Hawaii Hall

+ **Ficus religiosa, Bo Tree**
Foster Botanic Garden

○ **Garcinia mangostana, Mangosteen Tree**
3 in grove, Kaneohe Ranch

Guazuma tomentosa, Guacima Tree
Grounds of State Department of Agriculture
1428 South King Street

Hernandia ovigera, Jack-in-a-box Tree
University of Hawaii, Manoa campus, mauka-ewa
side of Sinclair Library

Hibiscus tiliaceus, Hau Trees
Halekulani Hotel, sea side of dining room

+ **Hyphaene thebaica, Doum Palm***
Foster Botanic Garden

Kigelia pinnata, Sausage Tree
1071 Young Street

Kigelia pinnata, Sausage Tree
115 Kuukama Street, Kailua

Kigelia pinnata, Sausage Tree*
Coast Guard Station, Kalanianaole Highway

+ **Lagerstroemia speciosa, Queen Flower Tree***
Foster Botanic Garden

○○ **Litchi chinensis, Lychee Tree***
Walker Garden

○ **Litchi chinensis, Lychee Tree**
Kaneohe Ranch

+ **Lonchocarpus domingensis, Guama Tree**
Foster Botanic Garden

○○ **Macadamia integrifolia, Macadamia Nut Tree***
Walker Garden

Mammea americana, Mammee Apple Tree*
Grounds of State Department of Agriculture
1428 South King Street

○○ **Mangifera indica, Mango Tree**
Walker Garden

○○ **Manilkara zapota, Chicle Tree***
Walker Garden

Manilkara zapota, Chicle Trees
two trees, 1071 Young Street

+ **Manilkara zapota, Chicle Tree**
Foster Botanic Garden

○ **Metroxylon carolinensis, Ivory Nut Palm***
grove of five, Kaneohe Ranch

+ **Mimusops elengi, Pogada Tree**
Foster Botanic Garden

Pandanus odoratissimus, Red Hala Tree*
Swanzy Beach Park

Peltophorum inerme, Yellow Poinciana Tree
Queen's Medical Center

○○ **Phyllanthus emblica, Indian Gooseberry Tree***
Walker Garden

Pithecellobium dulce, Opiuma Tree*
Fernhurst, 1566 Wilder Avenue

+ **Pritchardia macrocarpa, Dwarf Loulu Palm***
Foster Botanic Garden

Prosopis pallida, Kiawe Tree
1071 Young Street

Pseudobombax ellipticum, Pink Bombax Tree*
Queen's Medical Center

○○ **Psidium cattleianum f. lucidum, Waiawi Tree***
Walker Garden

Pterocarpus indicus, Narra Tree*
Tantalus Drive—on curve near pole #3665

++ **Roystonea oleracea, Cabbage Palm**
Harold L. Lyon Arboretum

+ **Roystonea oleracea, Cabbage Palm**
Foster Botanic Garden

Roystonea regia, Royal Palms
Both sides of Royal Palm Drive, Wahiawa

○ **Roystonea regia, Royal Palms***
30 lining old carriage road, Kaneohe Ranch

Samanea saman, Monkeypod Tree
420 Wyllie Street

Samanea saman, Monkeypod Tree
Central Union Church, courtyard of Atherton Chapel,
1660 South Beretania Street

Samanea saman, Monkeypod Trees
along Paki Avenue, Kapahulu to Monsarrat Avenues

Samanea saman, Monkeypod Trees*
Moanalua Gardens, 1352 Pineapple Place

Samanea saman, Monkeypod Tree
1070 Aalapapa Drive, Lanikai

Santalum freycinetianum, Sandalwood Tree
behind Tripler Hospital

Sapindus saponaria, Soapberry Tree
Ala Moana Park

+ **Spondias mombin, Hog Plum Tree**
Foster Botanic Garden

Sterculia apetala, Panama Tree
Ala Moana Park

Sterculia foetida, Skunk Tree*
University of Hawaii, Manoa campus,
ewa-makai corner of George Hall

Sterculia urens, Nawa Tree*
Queen's Medical Center

Swietenia mahagoni, Mahogany Trees*
along Kalakaua Avenue between Beretania Street
and Kapiolani Boulevard

○○ **Swietenia mahagoni, Mahogany Tree**
Walker Garden

Tamarindus indica, Tamarind Tree
1071 Young Street

Tamarindus indica, Tamarind Tree
Judiciary Building, Ewa Courtyard

+ **Terminalia catappa, False Kamani Tree**
Foster Botanic Garden

○○ **Thespesia populnea, Milo Tree***
Walker Garden

County of Kauai

Adansonia digitata, Baobab Tree
Koloa Missionary Church

Albizzia lebbeck, Siris Tree
Gay residence, Waimea

Araucaria columnaris, Cook Pine Trees
Kipu Ranch

Calophyllum inophyllum, Kamani Tree
Waioli Mission House grounds

Cocos nucifera, Coconut Palm Grove
Coconut Plantation Marketplace

Durio zibethinus, Durian Tree*
Grove Farm Homestead Museum

Enterolobium cyclocarpum, Earpod Tree
Kauai Mortuary, Koloa

Eucalyptus robusta, Swamp Mahogany Trees*
Maluhia Road

Ficus microcarpa, Chinese Banyan Tree
Menehune Gardens

Ginkgo biloba, Ginkgo Tree
Kokee State Park

Pithecellobium saman, Monkeypod Tree
Gulick-Rowell home, Waimea

Terminalia catappa, Tropical Almond
Ahukini Road and Kuhio Highway

* *Text with illustration*
+ *Foster Botanic Garden, 180 North Vineyard Boulevard*
++ *Harold L. Lyon Arboretum, 3860 Manoa Road*
○ *Kaneohe Ranch, Maunawili*
○○ *Walker Garden, 2616 Pali Highway*

Note:
*Nomenclature is that legally recorded on the official registers;
recent changes have not been noted.*
*Copies of the State law protecting trees may be obtained from
the State Library, see: "Session Laws of Hawaii 1975."*
*Copies of the Protective Ordinances are available at City
Clerk's offices.*

10

Red Hala Tree

Pandanus odoratissimus

For centuries islanders around the Pacific have obtained many useful items from hala trees flourishing in Hawaii and other parts of the Pacific. There are both male and female hala trees. Male hala trees bear an abundance of drooping white flowers hanging from clustered stems. A pale green fruit resembling a miniature pineapple grows on the female hala. It divides into solid sections that normally turn first deep yellow and then orange or red as the fruit ripens. Mature hala trees are characterized by stilt-like props of aerial roots on their trunks.

In old Hawaii sleeping mats, pillows, sandals, and outrigger canoe sails were among the objects woven from dried lau hala, the leaves of the tree. Fans, baskets and attractive handbags are made from the leaves today. A lei made from the brightly colored fruit sections is often worn by those of Hawaiian descent on New Year's Eve.

Hala, as the tree is called in Hawaii, is a member of the widespread Pandanus family whose species range from sea coast to mountain top in subtropical and tropical lands. Because of the conspicuous spiral arrangement of its leaves European sailors in the Pacific called the tree 'screwpine.'

The exceptional hala tree shown here at Swanzy Beach Park on windward Oahu is a very rare variety now in Hawaii. In old Hawaii leis of red hala fruit sections were only worn by alii—members of the ruling class.

Royal Poinciana Tree
Delonix regia

In spring and early summer the Honolulu skyline
is ablaze with hot orange to deep scarlet colored
treetops, as the city's many royal poinciana trees break
into fiery bloom. Delightfully, this tree flowers for
about six months of the year, looking its best in
summer.

The 'ōhai-'ula, as Hawaiians call the tree, is a
native of Madagascar. It was brought to Hawaii in
1855, most probably by Dr. William Hillebrand. A
rapid grower, it is a tough, wind-tolerant tree that can
stand drought and harsh conditions. For this reason
and because of its great beauty, the 'flamboyant,' as it
is known to Europeans, has been introduced to many
countries around the world.

The exceptional tree shown here is the largest of
its kind in the United States. It grows in the front yard
of a house built in the 1880's by W.G. Irwin on the
grounds of what is now Kaneohe Ranch on windward
Oahu.

Breadfruit Tree

Artocarpus incisus

Intrepid navigators from Tahiti brought the first breadfruit to Hawaii centuries ago. 'Ulu is the name Hawaiians gave to this luxuriant tree that originated in Malaysia and now grows abundantly throughout tropical Asia and Polynesia. The breadfruit shown is a mature tree that has been growing on the grounds of Kaneohe Ranch, midway between Honolulu and the windward side of the island, for decades.

Breadfruit is the most valuable food source among members of the Fig family, which also includes banyans. The large round fruit it bears has a green, warty rind. Rich in carbohydrates, it tastes much like sweet potato when cooked. No luau in the islands is complete without baked or steamed breadfruit.

In old Hawaii the light wood of the breadfruit was used for drums, door frames and canoe hulls. The sap provided a gum with which to trap birds prized for their colorful feathers. The distinctively shaped leaves of the breadfruit have been immortalized in Hawaiian quilt patterns and contemporary logos.

A quest for breadfruit to plant as a food source for African slaves in the British West Indies led Capt. William Bligh to make his historic voyage into the South Pacific aboard the HMS Bounty in 1788. Breadfruit trees may be seen in many island gardens.

14

Mammee Apple

Mammea americana

Alexander Adams, a Scottish sea captain who became skipper of King Kamehameha I's merchant ship *Kaahumanu* in 1816, introduced this fruit-bearing native of the West Indies to Hawaii. The bitter rind of the fruit that gives the tree its name encloses sweet-tasting orange flesh that can be eaten raw and cooked or made into preserves.

The mammee apple shown here, on the grounds of the State Department of Agriculture on King and Keeaumoku streets, is the largest of its kind in the United States. A handsome tree with lustrous, dark green foliage, the mammee apple is a member of the Mangosteen family. It grows in some private gardens in Hawaii.

15

Skunk Tree

Sterculia foetida

This otherwise attractive tree is named quite aptly for the staggering odor emitted by its pretty flowers, which are wine red tinged with orange and yellow. A native of the tropics of the eastern hemisphere, it has an unusual fruit that cracks open to expose black seeds resembling olives. When roasted the seeds are pleasant-tasting but have a purgative effect.

The exceptional tree shown here is on the University of Hawaii campus at Manoa near George Hall. It was planted in 1928 in honor of Liberty Hyde Bailey, an eminent horticulturist and botanist who was a world-renowned authority on palms as well as many other trees and plants. It is one of two skunk trees on the campus; the other is in front of Sinclair Library.

Many fine trees grow on the University of Hawaii campus. In 1918 Joseph F.C. Rock, the noted botanist and authority on native Hawaiian trees who taught at the University, recommended that a botanical garden be established on campus. Today dozens of trees planted by famous visitors to Hawaii, graduating classes, and as memorials beautify the grounds. Those designated exceptional include bo, cannonball, Jack-in-the-box, rubber and skunk trees.

Ironwood Tree
Casuarina equisetifolia

Archibald Cleghorn, father of Princess Kaiulani, heir apparent to the throne of Hawaii, planted this impressive double row of ironwood trees as a windbreak at the Diamond Head end of Ainahau, his Waikiki estate, in 1890.

As its name indicates, ironwood is very hard, but because it cracks and splits easily, it is not useful for building. A member of the Casuarina family, named for the Australian cassowary bird whose tufted feathers its needles resemble, the ironwood thrives in saline swamps near the sea. It is widely distributed in the Pacific from Australia to Malaysia. It was introduced to Hawaii in 1882 when Paul Isenberg, a German-trained agriculturist who founded several sugar plantations on Kauai, planted ironwood trees at Kilohana, Kauai.

Among the most interesting of several Pacific legends about the tree is one from Tahiti where ironwood is called toa, or warrior. Tahitians believe the tree sprang from the bodies of slain warriors whose blood became the tree's red sap, their hair the leaves. Other names for ironwood include beefwood, after the red coloring of its wood, and she oak, possibly after the soft sounds its needles make in the wind.

Swamp Mahogany

Eucalyptus robusta

The drive along Maluhia Road to Koloa and Poipu on Kauai is seldom forgotton by visitors or residents because of a striking tunnel of trees shading three-quarters of the road below Knudsen Gap. The trees are swamp mahogany, a variety of Eucalyptus introduced to Hawaii in the 1880's, which is now the most widely planted timber tree in the islands. The unusual arrangement of trees on this road was begun in 1911 when they were planted under the auspices of Walter McBryde, then manager of Kauai Pineapple Cannery. McBryde had 900 trees left over from landscaping the area around his home—now Kukuiolono Park. He and county engineer Joseph H. Moragne devised a plan for using some of the extra trees along either side of the new road being built at the time. Many Kauai residents helped plant the trees.

Dwarf Loulu Palm

Pritchardia macrocarpa

This striking palm with broad fan-shaped leaves is a rarity. Although it is small, it is over 100 years old, having been planted sometime after 1851 by Dr. William Hillebrand on the grounds of his private residence, now known as Foster Botanic Garden.

The dwarf loulu belongs to the only genus of palms native to the Hawaiian Islands. Over 20 species found nowhere else in the world have been identified. A single species is sometimes confined to one valley on a single island in Hawaii.

The original habitat for the dwarf loulu was the upper end of Nuuanu Valley on Oahu, above Foster Botanic Garden. It is thought to be extinct in the wild.

Hawaiians called this palm loulu (pronounced low-loo), which means umbrella, because the leaf formerly was used for protection from rain or sun; other uses were for thatching and basketry. The wood of some loulu palms were used for making battle spears. The seeds, when sanded and polished, make beautiful necklaces.

Cashew Nut Tree

Anacardium occidentale

The savory cashew nut is borne partially protruding from an edible, bright orange fruit called the cashew apple. The tree on which it grows is a member of the Mango family, which also includes poison ivy. Cashews, mangos and poison ivy have one thing in common; they exude an oil that can cause a painful rash or blister on susceptible skins.

The cashew nut tree shown here grows at Kaneohe Ranch on windward Oahu. It was cultivated by W.G. Irwin, turn-of-the-century owner of what was then Maunawili. He hoped to develop the cashew as a potential cash crop for the islands.

In India, where the majority of cashew nuts imported into the United States are harvested, the fruits are picked by hand and roasted, then the inner shells broken open by hand and the kernels heated to remove the skins. Understandably, cashew nuts never caught on commercially in Hawaii: labor costs would be too high. An attractive ornamental tree, the cashew is a native of tropical Central and South America.

21

Baobab Tree
Adansonia digitata

When God created the baobab, He first placed it on the hot plains of Africa. The baobab was dissatisfied with this choice and begged God to be replanted in the cool mountains. Soft-heartedly, God complied. But the choosy baobab didn't like the mountains either and asked to go back to its original home. Exasperated, God returned the baobab to the plains—upside down. That, according to African legend, is why the baobab has such a fat trunk and skinny branches.

The baobab at Queen's Medical Center on Punchbowl Street in Honolulu has a circumference of nearly 18 feet and is recognized by the American Forestry Association as the largest of its kind in the United States. It is among the trees believed to have been planted around 1859 when Queen's Hospital opened, by Dr. William Hillebrand, its first director. Other baobab trees may be seen in Ala Moana Park, Foster Botanic Garden, at the University of Hawaii campus, Manoa and elsewhere in the islands today.

A member of the Bombax family, the baobab bears dark green leaves and a large white flower with a slightly disagreeable fragrance. It develops a long woody fruit that from a distance looks like a large rat hung by its tail—hence a nickname, the dead rat tree.

In its native Africa the baobab's fleshy trunk is a water reservoir that swells to great girth during the rainy season and shrinks in the dry season when elephants sometimes strip off large pieces of its juicy bark. The swelling and shrinking process does not occur in the islands where there is sufficient water year 'round.

Hawaii's baobabs are very young. On the grassy plains of East Africa the baobab may live to be over a thousand years old. There, the hollowed out trunks of older baobabs are used as homes, for storage, as temporary prisons and burial sites. A strong fiber from the bark is made into rope and cloth. The baobab is grown as a curiosity in many warm climates around the world.

23

Milo Tree

Thespesia populnea

In pre-European times milo was a popular coastal shade and flower tree in Hawaii. The house of King Kamehameha I in Waikiki was surrounded with milo trees.

A native of the coasts of tropical Asia and the Pacific islands, the milo produces yellow, bell-shaped flowers that fade to pink soon after they bloom but remain on the tree for several days, creating a showy effect. In old Hawaii the fine-grained wood of the milo tree was made into calabashes. Today it is used for carving figurines and in other detailed woodwork.

The exceptional milo tree shown here, at Walker Garden in Nuuanu Valley, probably is the oldest tree on the grounds. It is believed to have been planted in the latter half of the nineteenth century when the garden was owned by High Chiefess Kekauonohi.

The milo is a member of the Hibiscus family. It is known as portia in other parts of the world.

Kamani Tree
Calophyllum inophyllum

The handsome low-branching kamani probably was introduced to Hawaii by people from other Pacific islands during an extensive period of migration that began over a thousand years ago. In old Hawaii its fine-grained wood was used for calabashes, and the oil from the nut within its small green fruit was used for lighting, and for rubbing down canoes. Dried, its fragrant flowers were used to scent stored kapa (cloth).

The spreading grove of exceptional kamani trees shown here at Kualoa Beach Park on windward Oahu is very old. It is said that the kamani was planted wherever a heiau (temple) for royalty was built.

A member of the Mangosteen family which includes the mammee apple, the kamani grows along the shores of lands bounded by the Indian and Pacific oceans. An evergreen, it is also known as Alexandrian laurel.

Kamani, Kualoa Beach Park

Brazil Nut Tree

Bertholletia excelsa

The tough-shelled Brazil nut is doubly protected from impatient monkeys and other predators in the jungles of its native Amazon Basin in South America. If the thick-walled seed pods are picked green, it takes an ax or other sharp tool to open them before the up to two dozen tightly packed nuts inside can be reached. But once ripe, the bottom portion of the pod containing the nuts drops to the ground, leaving the lid on the branch. Then, only the hard bony shells of the bland-tasting nuts must be cracked.

A large tree, the Brazil nut has leathery, bright green leaves and bears cream-colored flowers; it may grow to be 150 feet tall. The medium sized exceptional tree shown here at Walker Garden in Nuuanu Valley probably was planted around the turn of the century. A tropical tree, the Brazil nut is rare in the islands; this may be the only mature tree in Hawaii.

Mountain Apple

Eugenia malaccensis

The red, bell-shaped fruit borne in summer by this exotic member of the Myrtle family tastes like a crunchy honeydew melon or pear. It is a delight to hikers, who sometimes encounter groves of the trees in mountainous areas of the islands. A woodsy smell adhering to the tree makes picking and eating a fresh mountain apple that much more enjoyable. Bright cerise-colored flowers that look like pompons precede the production of fruit and make the mountain apple a popular ornamental tree, too.

A native of Asia, the mountain apple grows throughout the Pacific; it has been in Hawaii since pre-European times when it probably was introduced by migrating Polynesians. Hawaiians call it the 'ōhi'a-'ai. In old Hawaii its fruit was preserved by splitting it open to allow it to dry in the sun.

The mountain apple shown here grows in a shady spot on the grounds of Kaneohe Ranch, midway between Honolulu and Kailua. Many good sized trees grow along trails at Sacred Falls State Park in Punaluu.

29

Bo Tree
Ficus religiosa

This lovely, long-lived tree is honored in Hawaii and elsewhere for its role in the life of Buddha, who achieved enlightenment beneath a bo tree. A small rooted cutting from the oldest known historical tree, planted in 288 B.C. in what is now Sri Lanka, was sent to Mary Robinson Foster of Honolulu around the turn of the century. That tree now grows in Foster Botanic Garden in downtown Honolulu.

The tree shown here, the largest of its kind in the United States, is in Moanalua Gardens, on the way to Pearl Harbor. Other bo trees designated exceptional flourish at Walker Garden in Nuuanu Valley and on the University of Hawaii campus in Manoa. The tree at the University of Hawaii was planted in 1912 by the first graduating class from a cutting obtained from the Foster Botanic Garden tree.

In its native India, where it is called peepul, this handsome tree is sacred to Hindus who believe it to be the abode of the goddess Bhawani who can bestow fertility. Those who want children gather around a tree on Saturday mornings to petition her favor.

A member of the Fig family, the bo has long-stemmed, heart-shaped leaves that flutter in the breeze. It is planted near Buddhist temples and frequently appears symbolically in both Buddhist and Hindu arts.

Geometry Tree

Bucida buceras

Hawaii residents whimsically call this popular tree the geometry tree. No doubt the angular, tiered aspect of its branching pattern reminded gardeners of a school assignment in geometry. In its native Panama, the West Indies and elsewhere it is known as the jucaro tree.

A salt-tolerant, seaside tree, its dense foliage has made it a common ornamental, as well as tubbed specimen, in Florida and Hawaii. Locally it also is prized as a lazy man's bonsai because its rapid growth allows easy trimming and shaping. In Puerto Rico, where it is abundant, its very hard, heavy yellow wood is used for carts, gates, fences and rural construction.

The geometry tree bears inconspicuous greenish-white flowers on spikes at the ends of its branches. They are followed by slightly larger inedible fruits. It is a member of the Terminalia family which includes the false kamani. The exceptional tree shown here is in Ala Moana Park.

31

Pink Bombax Tree

Pseudobombax ellipticum

Dr. William Hillebrand, the first director of The Queen's Hospital in Honolulu, was a noted botanist who introduced many trees to Hawaii. Among the most beautiful is one he planted on the front lawn of the hospital on Punchbowl Street now known as Queen's Medical Center.

The pink bombax, a tropical American tree, is starkly leafless in winter, but in spring the showy tree is covered with huge clusters of brilliant pink blossoms. If you stand beneath the tree at the right time in January or February you can hear the long buds of its flowers pop open. The five pink petals of the bud curl back to expose a puff of long rose-colored stamens joined at the base. Their appearance has given rise to another name for the bombax used elsewhere than in Hawaii—the shaving brush tree.

Durian Tree

Durio zibethinus

When King Kalakaua of Hawaii made a trip around the world in 1881, seedlings of trees suitable for fruit bearing and economic use were sent back on his behalf from many different nations. Among them were some obtained in Borneo of the extraordinary durian tree, famed for a fruit that smells terrible but has a tantalizing taste.

Planted by George N. Wilcox, 'King Kalakaua's Durian' thrived and now is about 50 feet tall. The heavy, greenish-yellow fruit it bears is football shaped and covered with forbidding, somewhat woody prongs. Although the smell of a ripe durian, as the fruit is called, seems unendurable, the taste of the creamy pulp inside it is delicious.

A member of the Bombax family, the durian is cultivated for its fruit in the Philippines, Thailand, Indonesia and Malaya. It is rare in the United States. The tree shown, at Grove Farm Homestead Museum on the island of Kauai, bears fruit intermittently.

Banyan Tree
Ficus benghalensis

An array of aerial roots that develop into additional trunks makes this an easily recognizable tree in gardens and parks all around Hawaii. Native to tropical Asia, the banyan grows to heights of about 100 feet. Its multiple auxiliary trunks frequently make it even wider. In the Calcutta Botanic Garden in India there is a banyan tree with so many trunks it takes ten minutes to walk around it.

In Hawaii several notable banyans shade residents and visitors. Those shown here are on the grounds of 'Iolani Palace, and in the courtyard of the Sheraton Moana Hotel in Waikiki. Both trees are over a hundred years old.

The banyan at 'Iolani Palace once was two trees between which carriages drove to bring guests to visit King Kalakaua in the 1880's. Additional roots have bridged the gap since then.

During a lengthy stay in the islands, English poet Robert Louis Stevenson wrote a poem beneath a Waikiki banyan for lovely young Princess Kaiulani, heir apparent to the throne of Hawaii, who had left the islands to visit Europe.

> *Her islands here in Southern sun*
> *Shall mourn their Kaiulani gone,*
> *And I, in her dear banyan shade,*
> *Look vainly for my little maid.*

Together with the fig and breadfruit, the banyan is a member of the Fig family. Its common name is derived from the Banians, Hindu traders who used to camp in the cool shade cast by the tree.

The banyan is sacred to Hindus because it is believed that Brahma was transformed into a banyan tree. In the Marquesas Islands of southern Polynesia a banyan sometimes occupies a place of honor at one end of a chief's house.

Banyan, ʻIolani Palace

Queen Flower Tree

Lagerstroemia speciosa

When it is in bloom, this is one of the loveliest flowering trees in the world. A native of southeast Asia, ranging from India as far south as Australia and north to the Philippines, it is crowned with showy lavender blossoms, an annual process that begins when it is as small as six feet in height. Hawaiians call it the Kahili Flower because its blossoms are clustered together at the end of long branchlets. These resemble kahili, the tall staffs topped with feathers used to indicate the presence of royalty in old Hawaii.

In India heavy logs of the Queen Flower Tree are removed from forests by elephants. Used for general construction, the wood is considered second only to teak in quality. At 62 feet, with a spread of over 50 feet, the exceptional tree shown here in Foster Botanic Garden is the largest of its kind in the United States.

Kauri Tree

Agathis robusta

The largest living tree in New Zealand is a kauri with an immense girth of 55 feet estimated to be between 3500 and 4000 years old. The towering tree shown here at Foster Botanic Garden is a Queensland kauri, an Australian variety of the native New Zealand tree. The largest tree of its kind in the United States, it is a mere 105 feet high and has a girth of only 17 feet. It was planted sometime after 1851 by Dr. William Hillebrand who was seeking potential sources of timber for the fledgling ship building and repair industry in Hawaii.

The kauri is a member of the ancient Araucaria family that was widespread on the earth over 65 million years ago. It is valued for its fine white straight-grained wood and is an important source of copal, a key ingredient in varnishes and printing ink. Copal is collected from the resin of living trees or is dug from the ground as a fossil. Early settlers in New Zealand discovered enormous deposits of the fossilized resin occupying over two million acres of land. Another exceptional kauri tree in Hawaii may be seen at Lyon Arboretum in Manoa Valley.

Cannonball Tree

Couroupita guianensis

Dozens of round, rust-colored balls about the size of large grapefruit are clustered around the trunk of this soft-wooded tree in Foster Botanic Garden. Odder even than the 'cannonballs' is the flowering style of this native of northeastern South America. It bears large fragrant blossoms that spring from small branchlets protruding directly from the trunk of the tree. The highly fragrant flowers last only one day and are followed by the 'cannonballs,' which take about 18 months to mature. When these fall to the ground ripe, they give off a pungent, unpleasant odor.

The exceptional cannonball tree, the largest of its kind in the United States, is in Foster Botanic Garden. It bears showy, salmon-colored flowers. A younger tree nearby bears burgundy-red flowers. A member of the Brazil Nut family, the cannonball tree is nearing extinction in the wild. Another exceptional cannonball tree, planted by *Our Town* playwright, Thornton Wilder, may be seen on the makai side of Sinclair Library at the University of Hawaii at Manoa.

Indian Gooseberry Tree

Phyllanthus emblica

The translucent fruit of this prettily branching tree has a high vitamin C content and, like the widely grown gooseberry on the United States mainland, may be made into preserves that offset its sour taste. In its native Sri Lanka, Malaya and India, a fermented drink made from the fruit is used to cure coughs and other ailments. Tannin in the leaves, bark and fruit is extracted for tanning purposes.

The tree shown here is on the grounds of Walker Garden in Nuuanu Valley. It probably was planted around the turn of the century. Grown as an ornamental, the Indian gooseberry is rare in Hawaii; this tree is the largest of its kind on Oahu.

42

Doum Palm

Hyphaene thebaica

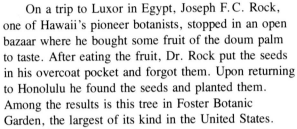

On a trip to Luxor in Egypt, Joseph F.C. Rock, one of Hawaii's pioneer botanists, stopped in an open bazaar where he bought some fruit of the doum palm to taste. After eating the fruit, Dr. Rock put the seeds in his overcoat pocket and forgot them. Upon returning to Honolulu he found the seeds and planted them. Among the results is this tree in Foster Botanic Garden, the largest of its kind in the United States.

The doum palm, native to upper Egypt and the Sudan, has been cultivated since earliest historic times for its fruit, which is reputed to taste like gingerbread, giving rise to another name for the tree—gingerbread palm.

The tree was sacred to the ancient Egyptians. It is easily recognizable in museum collections of Egyptian art by its unusual, dichotomous branching pattern.

Mindanao Gum Tree

Eucalyptus deglupta

The satiny trunk of this tall tree in Wahiawa Botanic Garden shimmers with color. If you stand close to it in the sunlight, iridescent shades of green, blue, lavender and rust play across its surface, as though deliberately to entrance you. A painter might see rich hues of Kelly green or burnt Sienna among the colors. School children in Hawaii like to call it their 'painted gum tree.'

Harold L. Lyon imported the first seeds of this tree from New Guinea in 1939. They were planted in what was then an experimental nursery maintained by the Hawaii Sugar Planters' Association. Although the tree, the largest of its kind in the United States, is now 90 feet tall, it is still young. Eventually it may grow to nearly 200 feet, about as tall as the Aloha Tower on Honolulu's waterfront.

Joseph Banks and Daniel Carl Solander, Captain Cook's botanists, on their voyage through the South Pacific in 1770 identified the large genus to which the Mindanao Gum belongs. Later, a French botanist gave the genus a Latin name, Eucalyptus, which means 'well-covered,' in reference to a protective cap atop the growing flower shed upon blooming. Over 600 species of Eucalyptus have been identified. Many provide prime lumber. In Hawaii they protect denuded watersheds and are planted as shields against trade winds.

The Mindanao Gum is one of only a few species of Eucalyptus not native to Australia. Indigenous to Davao, a province on the island of Mindanao in the Philippines noted for its huge rain forests, it ranges from the southern tip of the Philippines to Papua New Guinea. Another large example of the tree may be seen in Foster Botanic Garden. Small groves of it have been planted in many parks and public places on Oahu and the neighbor islands.

Waiawi Tree

Psidium cattleianum f. lucidum

A Spaniard, Don Francisco de Paula Marin, who landed in Honolulu in 1791, introduced the guava to island palates. An avid gardener, Marin grew many fruits and vegetables in a fertile plot on what is now Vineyard Boulevard in Honolulu. Among them was the guava, now enjoyed in jellies, jams, juice, ice cream, and even cake.

A native of tropical America, the shrubby tree that bears guava is grown commercially in Hawaii. It is common along roadsides and beside hiking trails.

The voluptuously shaped tree shown here in Walker Garden in Nuuanu Valley is waiawi or yellow cattley guava, a variety of the common guava. About 75 years old, it is the largest of its kind in Hawaii. Its fruit is bright yellow, in contrast to the strawberry-colored guava of the same species. A member of the Myrtle family, this guava is called waiawi by Hawaiians.

46

Wiliwili Trees
Erythrina sandwicensis

Four sisters once lived in Ka'u on the Big Island. The first, whose name was Moholani, was very beautiful. Unfortunately, the second sister was bald, the third was humpbacked, and the fourth had ragged, wind-tossed hair.

Beautiful Moholani married and had a son who was given to the gods to raise. One day Moholani's husband was lured out to sea by some pretty sirens. Frantically, Moholani asked her sisters to help find her errant husband. But they refused, calling him worthless. This aroused the wrath of Moholani's son who sent lightning to transform the sisters into wiliwili trees. The bald sister became a wiliwili with few leaves, the humpbacked sister a gnarled wiliwili and the wind-tossed sister a wiliwili with leaves that flutter in the breeze. Thus chastened, Moholani's husband returned, never to stray again. That, according to Hawaiian legend, is how the wiliwili tree came to be.

The habitat of this native Hawaiian tree is the dry leeward side of the islands from sea level to 2000 feet. It has gnarled, wide-spreading branches, long-stemmed leaves and spring flowers that range in color from pale red to white.

In pre-European times the buoyant wood of the wiliwili was used for surfboards, canoe outriggers and fishnet floats. Its red, oblong seeds were used in leis. The wiliwili trees shown here are remnants of an ancient grove inside Koko Crater Botanic Garden on leeward Oahu.

Pili Nut Trees

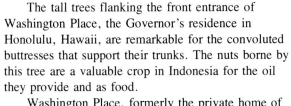

Canarium vulgare

The tall trees flanking the front entrance of Washington Place, the Governor's residence in Honolulu, Hawaii, are remarkable for the convoluted buttresses that support their trunks. The nuts borne by this tree are a valuable crop in Indonesia for the oil they provide and as food.

Washington Place, formerly the private home of Hawaii's last monarch, Queen Liliuokalani, was built by a Boston sea captain in 1846. Pili nut trees on the grounds appear in early drawings of the house together with fig trees. Possibly the sea captain or his son, John Owen Dominis, who became Liliuokalani's husband, had them planted. A native of Malaysia, the ornamental and useful pili nut is planted in rows along avenues in southeastern Asia.

Bunya Bunya Tree
Araucaria bidwilii

In 1857 a shipment from the Sydney Botanic Gardens to the 'King of the Sandwich Islands' arrived in Honolulu. Its contents included seedlings of this curiously shaped conifer, a member of the Araucaria family closely allied to pines, redwoods and other primitive trees. The seedlings were widely distributed on Oahu and the neighbor islands.

The aborigines of Australia gave the bunya bunya its common name. In its native habitat along the coasts of Queensland it bears large, pineapple-sized cones weighing up to ten pounds.

The tall bunya bunya shown here is on the grounds of Kaneohe Ranch on windward Oahu. It can be distinguished from the Norfolk Island Pine and other conifers native to the Southern Hemisphere by the 'all-mix-up' look of its branches, which are symmetrical on top but droop into an overlapping criss-cross below. Once prized in Hawaii and elsewhere for its wood, used for ship's spars and masts, it is now valued as an ornamental tree and often is cultivated as a potted plant. A tree, grown from one of the original seedlings to arrive in Hawaii, may be seen in Foster Botanic Garden.

Nawa Tree

Sterculia urens

This member of the Cocoa family, on the grounds of Queen's Medical Center on Punchbowl street in Honolulu, is recognized by the American Forestry Association as the largest of its kind in the United States. It was probably planted from seeds obtained by Dr. William Hillebrand sometime after his arrival in Hawaii in 1851.

The wood of the nawa tree is soft and light. In its native Asia the nawa yields karaya gum which is used as an adhesive agent in pill manufacture and as a thickener in sauces. Because they keep indefinitely, its soft, light tan leaves are popular in Hawaii for dried arrangements.

51

52

Kapok Tree

Ceiba pentandra

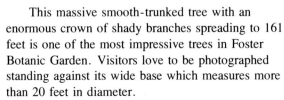

This massive smooth-trunked tree with an enormous crown of shady branches spreading to 161 feet is one of the most impressive trees in Foster Botanic Garden. Visitors love to be photographed standing against its wide base which measures more than 20 feet in diameter.

Dr. William Hillebrand introduced the kapok, a native of the tropics of the western hemisphere, to Hawaii sometime after 1851. The kapok tree shown here and a smaller kapok nearby are both well over 100 years old.

Many useful products are derived from different parts of the kapok. The most important is the buoyant fiber packed into the hundreds of large oblong seed pods produced by mature trees. The floss, called kapok, is used in life preservers and other water safety equipment. It can support 20 to 30 times its own weight in water. It also is used as stuffing for pillows and upholstery but because it is highly flammable use has decreased considerably with the development of modern synthetics. It still is an important export product in Java where the seeds in the pods are processed to obtain oil for soaps.

A member of the Bombax family, the kapok is native to tropical America but is now widespread, particularly in Asia and Indonesia, because of its usefulness. Another kapok tree designated exceptional on Oahu may be seen on the grounds of the State Department of Agriculture at King and Keeaumoku Streets.

Moreton Bay Fig

Ficus macrophylla

Between 1851 and 1857 shipments of seeds and seedlings from the Sydney Botanic Garden, addressed to 'The King of the Sandwich Islands,' arrived in Honolulu. Kamehameha III, who ruled Hawaii for thirty years—longer than any other monarch—and thus had time to consider his rapidly-growing dominion's needs, was the king to whom the new plants were sent. The exceptional tree shown here may be a legacy of one of those shipments, standing as it does on what was once a portion of the royal garden at Queen Emma Square in downtown Honolulu.

The small fruit borne by this native of Queensland and New South Wales, Australia, is tasteless, though attractive. A member of the Fig family, together with the banyan and breadfruit, it is an attractive ornamental tree.

Ivory Nut Palm

Metroxylon carolinensis

Sea captains traversing the Pacific in the 19th century frequently brought seeds and seedlings of new trees they encountered back with them to Hawaii in hopes of finding an eager buyer in need of a new source of food or timber. In a classic book written in 1917, *Ornamental Trees of Hawaii,* Joseph Rock reported that a Mr. Scott of Hilo, on the Big Island, purchased some strange-looking seeds from a ship's captain who had obtained them in the Caroline Islands in 1886. Resembling large, closed pine cones, but with a shiny, scaled surface, they contained a nut nearly as hard as a rock. Mr. Scott planted his seeds in Hilo. They sprouted the first Ivory Nut palm in Hawaii.

A native of the islands of Truk and Ponape in what is now Micronesia, the Ivory Nut palm was cultivated there for a time in the 19th century. Its seeds were exported to Germany as a vegetable ivory to make buttons. The tree shown here is one of five ivory nut palms among the great variety of exceptional trees at Kaneohe Ranch. It is thought to have been planted around the turn of the century. Another fine ivory nut palm may be seen in Foster Botanic Garden.

False Olive Tree

Elaeodendron orientale

This large ornamental tree in Foster Botanic Garden, the first of its kind in Hawaii, is over 110 years old. A native of Malagasy (formerly Madagascar) and Mauritius, it probably was planted from seeds obtained by Dr. William Hillebrand between 1851 and 1871. An attractive garden tree, it is prized for its handsome dark green juvenile leaves with mahogany red stripes. It often is grown as a tubbed specimen.

Opiuma Tree

Pithecellobium dulce

This pleasant street or garden tree, also known as Manila tamarind or Madras thorn, was given the name 'opiuma' by Hawaiians when it was introduced to the islands from its native tropical America. With its low spreading branches, the drought resistant, easy growing opiuma is a valued ornamental tree. A member of the vast Bean family, its seeds have been distributed by birds in dry regions throughout Hawaii.

The tree shown here, a rare variegated form, is in front of the entrance to Fernhurst, the Young Woman's Christian Association residence on the corner of Wilder Avenue and Punahou Street in Honolulu. It is the first of its kind in Hawaii.

57

Quipo Tree
Cavanillesia platanifolia

This fast-growing native of Panama and Colombia has a smooth, pale trunk. A member of the Bombax family, it is related to the kapok, baobab and pink bombax. Its soft wood is much like that of another relative, the balsa, although it is less useful.

The huge quipo shown here, growing in Foster Botanic Garden, is over 60 feet tall and nearly 15 feet around. It is the largest of its kind in the United States.

The distinctive seed pods produced by the quipo have five, angled wings. When dried, they are much in demand for dry arrangements and holiday wreaths. The seed of the quipo germinates in the pod without touching the ground.

Sausage Tree

Kigelia pinnata

In parts of its native Africa this remarkable tree is held sacred, understandably, and portions of its odd fruit are made into a black dye. In the western world no special use of the tree is made by man. It is simply a joy to look at because it seems so improbable.

The 'sausages,' which hang in clusters from long stems suspended from its branches, are green at first but then turn brown. Inedible, they may reach three feet in length and weigh up to 15 pounds. As somehow seems to befit it, the sausage tree blooms at night, bearing large reddish purple flowers that last only until morning and emit an unpleasant earthy odor. In Africa the odor attracts bats who pollinate the tree. The velvety flowers, which hang on pendulous stems, are replaced by the 'sausages.'

The exceptional tree shown here may be seen at the U.S. Coast Guard Station on Kalanianaole Highway on the way to Hawaii Kai. Others may be seen in Ala Moana Park, on the University of Hawaii campus at Manoa and at other sites around Honolulu.

Monkeypod Trees
Samanea saman

The gorgeous spreading canopy of this native of tropical America shades avenues, gardens, lawns and parks all over Hawaii. A rapid grower, the monkeypod is one of the finest shade trees in the world, with leaves that open out by day to screen off the sun's powerful rays, and close at dusk, shedding dew and earning it another name—the rain tree.

The magnificent symmetrical spread of the monkeypod may reach to 100 feet. In spring its broad green top is dusted with tufted pink flowers. In winter straight dark seed pods dangle from the branches of this member of the Bean family.

Bowls, platters and carvings are fashioned from the fine-grained monkeypod wood. Most of those sold in Hawaii now are imported from the Philippines.

The tree shown here is one of several exceptional monkeypod trees on the grounds of Moanalua Gardens near Pearl Harbor. Other monkeypod trees designated exceptional may be seen at Central Union Church, on Paki Avenue near Diamond Head, and in front of a private home on Wyllie Street in Nuuanu Valley.

Norfolk Island Pine
Araucaria excelsa

There is no break in the symmetrical arrangement of branches on this towering conifer which stands beside a white frame house built in the 1880's by W. G. Irwin, a businessman and avid plant collector, on the grounds of what is now Kaneohe Ranch on windward Oahu.

A member of the ancient Araucaria family together with the bunya bunya tree and hoop pine tree, this is a native of the island off northern Australia from which it gets its name. Easily distinguishable by the cone-shaped balance of its branches, the Norfolk Island pine tree is used extensively for reforestation and is also a popular potted plant. It is grown commercially on the Big Island of Hawaii for sale as Christmas trees.

The first seedlings of Norfolk Island pines arrived in Hawaii from Sydney Botanic Garden in 1852 in a shipment addressed to the 'King of the Sandwich Islands.' Many tall Norfolk Island pine trees grow on Oahu and the neighbor islands.

Macadamia Nut

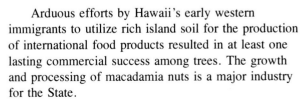

Macadamia integrifolia

Arduous efforts by Hawaii's early western immigrants to utilize rich island soil for the production of international food products resulted in at least one lasting commercial success among trees. The growth and processing of macadamia nuts is a major industry for the State.

E.W. Jordan, one of two brothers interested in horticulture, probably planted the first macadamia nut tree on Oahu at his Nuuanu Valley home around 1890. The tree had been introduced to Hawaii previously by E.W. Purvis, a member of King Kalakaua's staff, who planted macadamia nut trees on the Hamakua coast of the Big Island in 1885.

The macadamia, a native of Australia, bears its hard-shelled nuts in abundance throughout the year. Once the thick husks have been removed, the crunchy nuts within are roasted, buttered and salted. Delicious by itself, the macadamia is also the basis for many other tasty products made in Hawaii, from macadamia nut brittle to mouth-watering cream pie.

The exceptional macadamia nut tree shown here is on the grounds of Walker Garden in Nuuanu Valley. A member of the Protea family, the macadamia has dark green oblong leaves and a highly ornamental appearance.

Mahogany Trees
Swietenia mahagoni

The magnificent trees shown here growing along Kalakaua Avenue at the entrance to Waikiki were planted as ornamental shade trees in 1912 by The Outdoor Circle and the Forestry Department of the Territory of Hawaii. Seeds of mahogany trees had been sent to Hawaii from the West Indies by Gerrit P. Wilder in 1909. This was one of the first avenue plantings by The Outdoor Circle, which has since planted over 100,000 trees in parks, recreation areas and other public sites in the islands.

A native of the West Indies and the Florida Keys, this timber tree's fine-grained wood made it the most important material for elegant furniture made by English cabinetmakers in the 18th century. An evergreen, it has shiny, dark green leaves and small white flowers. It is grown on streets and for shade in many tropical countries. Another mahogany tree designated exceptional may be seen in Walker Garden.

Chicle Tree

Manilkara zapota

In tropical America the chicle tree is cultivated for its brown fruit with reddish flesh that is described variously as tasting like a peach in cream or a pear dipped in brown sugar. According to the owner of an exceptional chicle tree in Walker Garden in Nuuanu Valley, chicle fruit is delicious in fruit salad.

A member of the Sapodilla family, this evergreen was once the major source of the principal ingredient of chewing gum. For half a century, from 1890 until the 1940's, chicle trees in their native Central America were tapped for latex, largely for export to the United States. Synthetic materials are used in chewing gum today.

The reddish brown wood of the chicle is very strong and durable. The early Mayas used it for heavy construction and for carved lintels over temple doorways. Some of the carvings that have survived are over a thousand years old.

Several exceptional chicle trees grow in Hawaii; the one shown here is on the grounds of the Walker Garden. Another, the largest one in the United States, may be seen in Foster Botanic Garden.

Lychee Tree
Litchi chinensis

The khans of old Cathay dined on a small ambrosiatic fruit that looked like an oversized grape when it was peeled. Seeds for the tree, from which the extremely refreshing lychee came, first arrived in Hawaii in 1852 together with those of the longan, pomelo, Mandarin orange and other valued Oriental fruit trees. They were included in a shipment on board the first boat carrying contract laborers from southeast China to work on Hawaii's sugar plantations.

The lychee is a handsome, dense-foliaged tree that may produce more than 200 pounds of its rosy, thick-skinned fruit annually. The variety most prized in Hawaiian gardens is called kwai mi and has a small, easily removable pit.

The exceptional lychee shown here is on the grounds of Walker Garden in Nuuanu Valley; it is the largest of the seven lychee trees in the garden. The present owner likens the tree affectionately to a grizzly bear because of the rough appearance of its trunk.

Native to southern China and the Philippines, the lychee is a member of the Soapberry family. Dried lychee imported from Hong Kong may be purchased in Honolulu Crack Seed stores from Christmas through summer; canned lychee also is sold in supermarkets, but most Hawaii residents prefer fresh lychee.

Narra Tree

Pterocarpus indicus

The hard wood of this large-crowned timber tree is used extensively for fine hand-crafted furniture, panelling and cabinetry in its native Malaysia and in the Philippines, where it is honored as the national tree. Usually red or rose colored and sometimes variegated with yellow, it takes a high polish and has an enhancing rose-like odor. Much of the 'teakwood finish' furniture imported from the Far East is narra.

The exceptional tree shown here, growing on Tantalus Drive above Honolulu, is probably the first narra planted in Hawaii. A member of the Bean family, it bears fragrant yellow flowers followed by small winged seed pods.

Royal Palms

Roystonea regia

Cobblestones of the narrow road between these two rows of stately royal palms are buried beneath the green overgrowth on the grounds of Kaneohe Ranch in windward Oahu. Once they led from the old Waimanalo road up to a home owned in the last century by members of the Boyd family, who sometimes entertained their king, Kalakaua, and his younger sister, Princess Liliuokalani, there. In 1878, on a retreat to what was then known as Maunawili, the princess composed Hawaii's most famous song, *Aloha 'Oe*.

The first royal palm seeds were brought to Hawaii from the West Indies by Dr. Gerrit P. Judd, an advisor to King Kamehameha III, upon his return from a state visit to England in 1850. A native of the West Indies and tropical America, the royal palm is prized for the touch of elegance its stature lends to avenues and places of honor in the world. Two other rows of royal palms designated exceptional flank Royal Palm Drive in Wahiawa in central Oahu.

Index

Page numbers followed by ''p'' refer to photographs